Terra Incognita

POEMS BY

Adebe DeRango-Adem

Inanna poetry & fiction series

INANNA Publications and Education Inc.
Toronto, Canada

Canada Council **Conseil des Arts**
for the Arts **du Canada**

ONTARIO ARTS COUNCIL
CONSEIL DES ARTS DE L'ONTARIO
an Ontario government agency
un organisme du gouvernement de l'Ontario

The publisher gratefully acknowledges the support of the Canada Council for the Arts and the Ontario Arts Council for its publishing program, and the financial assistance of the Government of Canada through the Canada Book Fund.

Library and Archives Canada Cataloguing in Publication

DeRango-Adem, Adebe, 1986–, author
    Terra incognita : poems / by Adebe DeRango-Adem.

(Inanna poetry and fiction series)
Issued in print and electronic formats.
ISBN 978-1-77133-217-0 (pbk.). — ISBN 978-1-77133-219-4 (epub). — ISBN 978-1-77133-220-0 (pdf)

    I. Title. II. Series: Inanna poetry and fiction series

PS8607.E7145T47 2015   C811'.6   C2015-902268-1
                                                             C2015-902269-X

Printed and bound in Canada

Inanna Publications and Education Inc.
210 Founders College, York University
4700 Keele Street, Toronto, Ontario M3J 1P3 Canada
Telephone: (416) 736-5356   Fax (416) 736-5765
Email: inanna.publications@inanna.ca Website: www.inanna.ca

 MIX
Paper from
responsible sources
FSC **FSC® C004071**
www.fsc.org

For the itinerants and wanderers
for whom home is where the heart is
and all those in between.

Contents

…In the world through which [we] travel, [we are] endlessly creating [ourselves].

—Frantz Fanon, *Black Skin, White Masks*

ex-future

dear unborn children: your mulatta mama is sorry
for your loss/ couldn't figure out how to get ex-
coloured/ or be black no more/ needed to redeem myself
from the future/ and now I let days pass like quiet
drops of blood becoming rivers without song
and if you can't sing because you have no voice
I will teach you how to dance/ watch me/ thank me
for having at least imagined you into existence
given you the invisible life
which is what you would have gotten anyway
so let us dance together by the sea/ and underneath
the dirty fingernail moon/ follow me my sons and daughters
feel no gloom/ let your soul trouble the waters
be sea foam sometimes/ and other times be fire
or better yet be fire/ bringing water

full with arrival

You vastly yield yourself
when the distant call of birds
rings, and take it deep inside you,
feel bold, take all
the galaxies into your face.

Once, somewhere, I had set you free
with a sharp jolt, in an attempt
to tear myself away from youth,
approach greatness; but now I am home,
stand nakedly with a faint
strength attributed to womanhood
or a strong ribcage, give up
trying to recognize you
in the surging wave of
what must come next.

All the immense images in me
or of the me I had been,
far-off, in another kind of kinship,
I was once a powerful landscape,
pulsing with the life of the gods.

I used to fill men with arrival, bring the spirit
out of lived-in things. Nowadays
I fill others' hands differently,
with a kind of transactional return,
I show up.

Heavier by the weight of where they have been,
of what's already been prayed for.

my past lives

I was a rich sailor
in my first life,
and a tragic negress in the second

removed from sea or source
in my third life I decided
to become a gangster:
cigar smoke through bulletholes
and blondes

in this life it is
only breathing/darkness

light/darkness

sound/light

the shadows where hybrids hide
and h'aints keep hoping,
laughing in the veneer of gods

or maybe gods laughing
at the veneer of my face
but what science is there

what cosmology explains
the death of my language
lost to some New World bullshit

we are all growing in this World
preparing for our exit

the poem a memo
to remember us by

me, I've already died
in the chess fields of Harlem
on a hot jazzless night and come back
popping my fingers
to silence

mirror in place of veil,
ghost in place of flesh,
question mark for poem,
my last words a good long laugh

tools for prayer

I give you my mouth, hands,
give you the things
used for prayer and I give you
my prayer

I give you my northern love
to warm and to hold and confess that I feel
for the first time my body
leaving its winter

I give you a sense of literature, though my scripture
was inherited by your forefathers,
the ones you traded in for code
and look to tangentially

I give you my lips in the name of the father
and of celestial sun, the holy poetry
I hope will be the poetry of unveiling
and I give you my unveiling

I give you my holiness, the particular geometry
of my heart, I take off
into your chest,
come into you with reverence

I give you my reverence
see you in time and yet outside
of it, pause in the psalm
of your glory, hover in the open air

and you open me to the air
as I sail to you knowing
that quiet waters
do not make skilful sailors
and I am happy your body is not quiet

that it sings with the study of loving
and sings with loving;
for you I have opened the skies of myself,
if not for you the sky a finite thing.

my religion is language

after Charles Bernstein

I am learning to be the flower
instead of the rake, learning to stop
maiming my own viscera,
speak easy never, uproot, repent,
de-vein: I feel it might be my turn
to return to nature

so I chain these chains together, up and away—
I face my face and
name my name, I weather
the storm and storm the fire
by the subtle hum
of a fearful, hopeful
repair

and the myrrh may have marred
the ancient beauty of my face,
and there are still days I am
averse to grace, divine
that the divine is a lie

but anxiety is
nostalgia for the future
and fear of the past; I want instead
to turn my body into text, or let the text

of my body appear to be the inner
living of an outer dream,
or vice-versa
or just verses, mixed in with a little vice

whether there was light before language
matters little;
what we need are not the words
to describe the broken
glass but how the light dances
off the shards

in other words:

in a word, a whole world;
in the world, the Word.

dialectics

after Natasha Trethewey

I have waited
       my whole

life to see
       two half

blacks like me
       walk full and beautiful in the white

house singing to the poetry
       of everyone:

between you and me
       I suspect all angels

of history are also half-caste,
       phantoms that they are, and that history is.

weatherman

My father speaks
as a boy of motherless tongue,
the language of eternal hustle
suited up in a weary quickstep.
        Trudging in cadences of Romania
to Turkey, en route to New York
and then Toronto,
    where he would finally find the speech
of frantic muscular jazz birthed
in the concrete between trees,
        and eventually a home,
dialect of secret
societies, underground acronyms of men
buzzing with a dream.

My father makes the sound
of a perpetual question,
will stare you down into eternity,
the underworld of men who understand
blessing and always ask
where ya goin'
    and which places, if you ask him,
are recounted with joy,
beginning with a throat clearing, the battlefield
of his lungs, majestic

gestures moving at the speed of fire
        gullet bullet,
constant reminder—

       He will speak to you
in your third eye,
watch you as a weatherman preparing
for storm,
remind you of elementals
even without rain,
    fundamentals religion won't explain.

Elemental father
   who will mistake this poem
for a sleepy ode
having wanted only to burn
in the minds and eyes
of wanderers of generations
weary with worldliness
and rain,
        to listen for sunrise
speak poems
from his veins, bring me up always
and tell me to walk that way—
        chin up, eyes closed—
and when the light pours in
he will ask me to recount the colours,
always red, yellow, and green,

traffic colours, the colours
of movements and uprising.
With each game I understood
        spectrums, the struggle to find light.

His silhouette on certain mornings
as he'd leave to catch the 52 bus,
a white smoke cloud rising
from his black afro hair
        I am there

in the scenery always, saying bye under my breath
        but meaning to say
every poem is praise
and is where you are.

soul brother

I never had a brother nor
another mother
but from your baby photos maybe—who knows?—
in another universe I've known you

light skin kinky hair
soul of light my kin
from some historical night
or were you some historical knight

fighting for our future,
the kind of people we call black
or brown or
lack

the people who lack kin—
let's do a throwback:
you were never meant to work the fields
you were never meant for a field at all

your talents across moons and all
maroon shades of history:
you were a kid, once,
and my brother from another

but you are not my Other
and we are not Other

and we are also
not the same

but somehow and otherwise,
in some other paradise,
we are sister and brother—
you'd better believe it!

at least before the world
stops believing in the very power
our otherness
begets all of us

blood root

after George Elliott Clarke

I, too, am America,
have always been,
like you. But did you
feel something

more in the crawling
ivy, gathering like leagues
down the backs of black trees?
Did you gather the leaves?

    Blood on the leaves and blood at the root

Or did those trees merely point
heavenward, the real place
for our dreams,
aspirations made moot?

For the first time
in the history of these skins
the mulatto brother wins.
But what of the screams—

    Blood on the leaves and blood at the root

Not of bop, the language
of America's inevitable Africa;
but the stench of magnolias,
mixed with burning flesh.

And what of the buried heads between
clutched hands, black copper, eulogy?
The unredeemable skins
Of unredeemable fruit?

Blood on the leaves and blood at the root

dark continent

If Freud were right
and all women are dark continents
then maybe all men are ill
lands.

black russians

taste like my beloved:
Russians, dubbed the blacks of Europe—
       through him I see my shadow
       come to light:

       the rest is rust
       and stardust

a black hole of promise—
       I knew you were the one
       when I saw you walk calmly through the fire
       and scare away the dark

and it was then I prayed the flames
never completely bite the dust

my love,
when I look at you I am drowning
in the sky and stardust, and all rust
turns to gold

blues for Baraka, in memoriam

no spontaneous ignorance
you said to me that summer
in a hot room, holding pen and pencil
wearing glasses you'd rather smash

who will speak now of a beatific rising
hear the most radical heartbeat
reduced to echo, rickety chairs, breeze
who will follow your dialectic—

that of life itself, of a position neck to neck
with aesthetics, your conviction always
more blues than jazz:
Roll over, Beethoven

you wanted atonement, not Nietzsche;
you wanted feeling, mixed with funk;
you wanted that pesky thing called freedom
but you never wanted grace

now you join the rest without protest,
bearing a quiet face—
      who will burn now,
      who can do right by undoing…

I entertain these thoughts while waiting
not for the A train but any train,

remember the cries that came
from small workshop rooms

when you marched onto everyone's notebooks,
left the door deliberately ajar;
spoke in bleeding headlines,
need to get the story straight

now the room that I inhabit will be the night,
I will rehearse a last quatrain
on the next train out,
listening for your blazing light.

bastardette

I am your daughter, black man!
Nightfall
in these Canadian woods.

One of the pillars of the temple fell.

I am your daughter, like Hell!

The moon over the Canadian woods.
The Northern night
Full of stars,
Great big yellow stars.

What's a body but a ploy?
Black bodies,
playing in the dark.

The scent of pine wood stings the soft night air.

What's the body of your mother?

Silver moonlight everywhere.

What's the body of your mother?

Sharp pine scent in the evening air.

Mulatto night,
Mulatto whirl,
A little yellow mulatto girl.
Naw, you ain't my brother.
Not ever.
Dark bodies ain't my brother.

The Northern night is full of stars,
Great big yellow stars.

O, sweet as earth,
Dusk dark bodies
Give sweet birth

To little yellow bastard boys.

Get on back there in the night,
You ain't white

The bright stars scatter everywhere.
Pine wood scent in the evening air.

whose bloodline is it, anyway?

how do you enact a force of freedom
that can escape the temporality of my life?
make it into a music,
a black noise, an offering for Exu,
a drumbeat of bones—
poise your song into a set of words
that no one knows, musical lines
like blood lines that oppose
that cancel to reveal
that mystify to expose

Dante's *Girl at a Latrice, 1862*

my mouth repeating itself
into scream, into the eventual
constellations that vacationers would grow
to wish on,
we stared angrily from gutters
wondering how many prophets were killed
in the great silhouette of your strength,
how many of my mulatrices
died in the latrices
of your gloria mundi
your sweet face like Beatrice
transposed into an arrangement of points
a psychology orange and sad,
ornamenting itself in nights
when my great-great grandfathers
prepared their own soil;
what structure of you can hold
Huis Clos?
your gaze, behind iron lacing
imagining hell as other people
never right here

lady of the lakes

I remember you by:

long black stairs
a claw foot tub,
poppy seeds,
shoelaces to be learned by book,
a caged gypsy—though not quite caged,
just a sage in captivity,
caught in the artifices of the city,
of the Western world,
this uncomfortable earth
we can sometimes only bare
with the rough intuition
of toes on sand;
and you are also sand, your skin
kissed by lake,
water beneath a million dusks,
the place where I also became a mermaid
for good, where
I learned the meaning of

      sunset
      tea as a nightcap
      the tragedy of a fly's life span

the beauty of recognition
when the people you love love
what you do and when you do what you love

in order to become

        ocean
        lake
        bay
        river
        pond—

hot sand and stone beneath
the nubile sole hurts,
but that's how the soul gets through

marron inconnu

the sea gives me elemental warnings as I wait
for signs of promise, signs
of solitudes being broken down and
bodies growing by tremor into new birth
into a moment when our native land
stretches its arms and I become we
for are we all not somehow abandoned in spirit

this is how the sea compensates
for our chaos of forms
              for are we not all awaiting judgment
the great test of how we can keep still
and guarded against the storm of memory
that blurs our bodies against the wind
submerging the cliffs, the histories
history books escaped:
              blanc, mulatto, negre, marronage

our histories, songs of calypso
thrown into apocalypse,
tales blurred against the winds
submerged beneath cliffs,
whose people are ghosts, ghosts still sharp,
abandoning themselves
to Ayiti, Ayiti
where the romance of origins

was washed away by Louverture
and though now not many think
of his alpine death or his hands
bringing news of the end of la France
to assure the ancestors/exiles in their own soil
that there would be light,
        he is till traversing those waters
        alive and black
his overture gone
but underground we carry on.

everyone wants to be DuBois

everyone wants to be DuBois,
the voice of the next
generation

but what about the noise? the sound
of young black boys
hitting the ground

what about the toys the old boys
are using to bruise and end lives?
what about the ploys

to get the care we need and where
is my choice to be physically let alone
existentially free and how

do I establish
me—
I am not W.E.B. but I am

caught in a web of
doubt and dread; all I want is my people
to be free

but you see, from sea to shining sea

the colonial regime remains
unphased from sky to tree

Lord, or somebody, take the lead

in this time of need and era of greed,
I plead guilty
for wanting to believe

for standing my ground under this
shifting earth beneath my feet
and being misunderstood when I say I can't breathe…

I still see…
the void
as well as the beauty

can feel precisely, and can speak;
at the very least
these bones still creak

and when I get weak I can
still plead guilty to still wanting
to believe in this bleak

carnival called earth—
for what it's worth, I still want to learn
        and dance
        and burn
        and churn all waters
        that remain still

oltremare

where clean soil where undivided earth where water
without blood where siren song without scream where white
sand without darkness where yellow sun without blindness where fluid
river without memory where sea without nostalgia where ocean without
regret where waves without undertow where seashell without secrets
where compass without chaos where ship without wreckage where sailor
without drink where water without impurity where altar without church where
dusk without parting where reef without peril where treasure without loss
where mist without veil where oxygen without breathlessness where breath
without gasp where calm without departure where arrival without fear where
paradise without somewhere else where here, where how, where
fore art thou

dragging sea chests around the bend

The blur of desire's devising force and the divisions
we so acquire are always the gifts of either oblivion
or the opaque world of drink.
    Here the promise of night

is always already broken, already
about what could have been
or what shouldn't have.
    At least that's what I tell myself

on those man-made nights when the women
walk like makers but are truly the unmade.
It is the shadow of grace
    that keeps me coming here,

the shadow of something sleepless also,
and gold, the revelation
of something one already knows,
    the face of a perfect stranger

whose gaze makes you forgive.
There is never truly a decision, you must only
survey what is left, walk
with one foot in front
    of the other,

left, and right, smile the way

you might have as a child no matter where
you stand or lie
    as you may be doing now, in the anonymous

town squares of your adulthood,
your being mine.
Getting old means always taking leave;
    it is often a matter of a train

leaving,
hunks of metal blowing kisses of exhaust,
exhausted.
    It is always the locking of doors

attempts at escaping gravity
with stories of origin, root,
trying hard to transcend
    metaphysics,

reflect on your life in the old films,
those times when you might have been
Antony or Cleopatra
    lost in some eclipse of nations—

do you not remember?
It is a western longing now,
that cuts our caricatures into a vague purpose.

It is the sound of a motor and tires crunching snow,

it is our lives reduced to a poem about snow:
plain whiteness forever.
But whatever passes
    for chance also passes for truth.

This notion plainly suits me
like it should a traveler, moving
along a path lighted
    by what has survived.

to the yellowknife woman

you were yellow
of skin, abandoning
your chest, becoming
the warm waters, speaking a botched message
(a footprint in the imaginary snow)

and how icily, easily
you chose your Tiffany ring

I imagined you caressing
jewel after jewel in the dark,
while looking at the empty space
of your hand soon to be filled
with more glass and a faint
shade of smoke

imagined the empty space
of your land:
you were tough as tundra once,
but things change, we soften
with age and disappointment,
though our beauty fights to remain

our faces, too, an unknown territory,
warts and all
and wars

taciturn city

what, if not transformation,
if life's urgent command?
        I walk in praise of cities,
urging my urgent gate to kiss fully
the mouth of the night sky

I scatter myself wildly
into the night, unrepentant,
of the things I did
or will not do, breath merely the bridge
opening up across a river,
endless in its desire to live

my transformation the singing of praises
of no one in particular
        or everyone—
my own body
no more or less than soul,
        a perfect soliloquy,
        an attempt to communicate
in a mauve and trembling
realization that we may be forgotten
in the same skylines we reckon with

and yet our destinies
somehow not mammalian,
but the manifestations of light;
        I travel light

exploring the silent tutelage
or maybe sermon
of sticks and stones
whose mantra holds that every
heartbreak is a fiction,
a chance to reclaim—

discarding genealogy
I await, unmoored,
the benediction of the day
taking its first muscular breath,
        and should it fail to pour out its purpose
in vivid revelation I will
still rejoice, walk, tend to traffic
'lights as well as the craft
of every step

for who says each leaf that falls
on asphalt is no prayer

new world

The land that's yours is mine,
is shadows, which I see
both dreaming and in the night
when drums make our old selves dance,
bring us to embrace those old ghosts
weaving through. No one owns them
or us,
nor the fearful asymmetries
of our lineage, of our Caribe we left
for new callings, Kanata,
a new response
from Yoruba to Cuba we work hard
to reflect. This land that's yours
is a *patria* of *poes'a mulata;*
we shall not forget
these shanty towns, this Afroantillana
beyond the pale, beyond even Luis Palés Matos
and Nicolás Guillén there is a spirit
unlearning its colour and shade, becoming
the veil we pull out from the eyes,
becoming the spring reborn
again, peace of communion, landscapes
which fade at the edges but hold
our bodies in place, becoming letters

of pilgrimage, *terra nullius,*
becoming also the dark sea
that calls me to embark
into a dialectic of light and dark,
and then hopefully light again,
becoming the theories and poems
we wept for, and finally a true pledge for morning,
for the momentum to run, to sing
as a way of traveling, to await
only the moment where all that is static
shatters into hope.

ode to zong

O desire, O adventure, O nervous, tempestuous sea
        O fragile cosmos, *murmur of old men's voices*, O dialects
whose history Hegel could not understand.
        O Middle Passage I will never understand, but that gave me life.
Shuttles in the rocking loom of history,
        the dark ships move, the dark ships move.
Now, when people speak of voyage, they speak of mythic liberty.
        An empty ice box,
fantasy of plums. The ghosts of Celestino,
        poor mulatto, another cargo
down. When you've known bodies as jetsam,
        you learn other ways to pray
and how to swim, in case.
        We were born this way, and this strange.
Born to deceive, hope for rescue, plea,
        sing the song of liberty from sea to shining sea.
But where, how to be buried in a land that's free?
        Alas, we were born for the voyage specifically.
The constant undertow, flesh in place of soul, we moan
        a hallelujah behind the veil and then

*Italicized lines borrowed from Ezra Pound's "Cantos II" and Robert Hayden's "Middle Passage,"
respectively

terra incognita

unchartered seas/skins unknown
histories/sins
regions unmapped
bodies undocumented
          do not search for us in the ancient texts
or paraphernalia, we are *terres inconnues,*
have always been a people
to be discontinued

our body parts unknown,
thrown down to the *mare incognitum,*
we make our way to the remote corners
of the cosmos, worlds reserved
for the other, redraw maps
though we do not want to be fully explored

we want only to be remembered
instead of forced to enter the realm of incognito
gnosis, the realm of knowledge
that is merely teaching cognizance
of difference
of *terra pericolosa,*
of blackness, the trans-atlantic sea sickness

when our ghosts left Rome,
or the Pythagorean gore that preceded

our haunting and our lives—
the middle passage where I was born

where once upon a time maps
like skin meant nothing, the endangered species
was all of us, the mystery
not degradable, the Spirit
never sharp.

poemagogy

Traffic sweat drips
flashing whiz children with red lips
neon age, yellow hallways
no décor
just wind: the age of reason.

I tried to reason with a lamppost
whatcha burning for? so many dead stars
like you dizzying up the streets, hardly any room
unlike a galaxy

but it wasn't really a lamppost
and I wasn't reasoning;

it was the simple act of pressing
palm to palm to
grape white saintliness,
the point at which a light
is formed and carries you forever

when it does not take off
with the wind
but remains like a question

the psychodynamic arc
of city life, trapping and liberation

Parlafilms:

where we speak as through
destroyed, where we only desire
to become something new.

Constant toil in the life of art!
the assemblage
slaveships deathtrains nightclubs
Eeenough—
our reality (swallow)
too much, these bells
summon what enabled us to clash

first into the night
like palms
when we are strong
with the
not yet,
with the beauty of now

when we lift high
the banner of reason
to run across lines of flight,
of light, singing
how every life shall be a song
or certainly some sense of mattering

of being indivisible—that is the only desire

there is, to be enabled with passing
words that foam
like seas deep with dark

to reducible neither to the One
nor the multiple,
to become not you
or two, three four five
nor to add you to myself

for we have all
always been in motion:
our dimension is the same,
lovers are
just interlocutors in general,
radical disturbances

like subways, a kiss, a missed stop:
the shock of the encounter
when beauty exceeds
the limits of the rational

the unscripted sublimity
of the earth, this place
we inhabit on loan.

The dead poets keep telling me
anonymity is a lie, this city just another point
of departure

that desire is just sympathy, not filiation
that we are angels,
alloys, the wind

that our roots are rhizomes,
our lives *creatio ex amore,*
multiplicity is what borne the city
is what borne us, we are still being
birthed again, and up, and away

what they call paradise

these are second-hand words
they come to me from the other

from a land we have not visited
before but I know we have imagined—

neverland, no man's land,
no woman's land, no place to land

but it is over slight levitation, by the grace of grace
that lets us breathe this place

leave martyrdom to the weak and weary
do not fear the clearing of the storm

it itself is a kind of healing,
for nothing gets clean without rain

there is love throughout the seasons,
the dry sun and sundry of winter, falling leaves

and spring showers, summer's triumphant
flowers; the flora does it all

despite the pain of impermanence
for what else, my dear

but to fear fear and love love,
and try, if only for a while,

to mimic the dire resilience
of angels

m(y)other

to live is to be other
to be new with each new dawn
to choose waking over waiting
to call the future perpetual, your paradise here
to keep nothing perfectly stocked and never fear a door left open
to be like the stars, burning for others;
to live is to imagine other possibilities
is to acquire difference and not habit,
be the lighthouse or, conversely, the dark—light's nesting place,
for when the things you long for
become the things you give
that's also how the light gets in.

terra nuova/anchors a-weigh

a shattered visage or voyage or vision
makes up this water now
makes up this body now, and with a make-believe
face I make myself believe myself to be
fire bringing water
to the future

I was usually the other way around: firewater,
burning unreasonably, seasonally the same: cold feet, hot-headed,
feeling nothing besides remains
my being little else other than
what remains of the self when the other takes over

little else other than decay, colossal
wreckage, a bare sea, bone
dry with wet brain, sands
of the soul stretching
far far away

soon to become awry, an unbelievable,
unblessable mess

I had heard somewhere that
If you don't believe it
at least be open to receiving it,
or at least that's what the sirens said
as they swam and sung in

synchronicity, symmetry,
in other words
God

let go and let sky become sea
become sky and be good
to yourself

what a strange new carving out of space
I reckon with here, what a new
curvature of the cosmos
new inventory to explain

yet something still awaits
another kind of place
for a *terra firma* beneath the feet

but can you roll with it
either on the rocks or neat?
can you jive with the strangeness
of being alive

there is no easy way from the earth to the stars—yes—

just as coming down
might trick you
into the simplicity of settling for less,

for bread
alone, or worse, myth
to live off legends and love off romance and
dedicate one's poetry over decanters
of cheap wine

coming down and finding new ground might
make you love without discretion and
turn your passion cheap,
to a simple geometry of get up, bathe, go

so be careful if the sun becomes ubiquitous
on your skin or the gleam gets old
for you may one day find yourself
wandering about Rome or Abyssinia,
wondering about your place in antiquity
where all that glitters was gold

angels are rarer these days—yes—
and cathedrals make shadows
and churches choke
and smoke fills the ears of the universe
but the body is your land

your body is your land and you learn to walk
in it you choose to be under its weather or above it
you decide whether to rise above
or leave or arrive

and when you sleep to dream
it is in that simple breath
that new stars appear,
putting everything together

you are without windows and wild—yes—
your soul is glorious
and you will learn to package yourself
differently, learn the true and only meaning of travel: to return
again and again

you will come to know your compass
was nothing more than blood,
your journey the attempt to ensure edges
can touch without bleeding and
your geography still seething with the upturned
noses of history,
and nosy histories,
and who knows

I know only this:
your land may not be yours
but you are sovereign for now anyway

this is your land mass, your sun
perforating the rooms of your being

pray for the land within the land,
the one that knows how to fly

stormwater

When each step is a beautiful concavity
Of sand, the voyage becomes expertly smooth.
        Idle sand dunes, shadows of earth,
Suddenly the ghosts

Do not bother us with their
Scurrying despair. What we hear
        Are the half-living, who whisper *I am still here*
Trying to remember themselves,

How they were loved as memories,
Dark and westward.
        Stitching the horizon
Are the too-human dreams

Discussed lightly over lemonade afternoons,
haze. But what of the sharpness of mornings,
        The bite of the dead berating the hour,
What of the natural world

Unfurling like old bills,
trying to remember itself as value.
        But what of the arrivals
That are only practice
runs for departures, ascension.

Only we the living live without
Certainty, or maps. No nation

Lines of delineation
Are untroubled by the waters, or ideas.

How many years are there left to cross over
The ghosts ponder, sighing the way
                    Gospels do.
The appalling beauty of brotherhood,

Hearts aghast in camaraderie, commonality.
What gives sight is not what sets free.
                    Can there ever be a face
Without lines to remember, softly,

And without the need to suspect.
I think of the buried bodies laid
                    In the finality of shade,
The country and cities

That are not here to remember us,
Or remind us that we will become a form of ghost,
                    Wishing for real shape.
Time is a white lie, travel a veil.

Nations float. They are light stormwater,
Waves crashing into the impossible
                    Mesoamerica, fine lines between
What is lost and found.

sea star

For your entire generation, this is a period of intense research and discovery in areas that were heretofore considered mysterious, remote or taboo. The root causes for many complex occurrences will be unearthed due to the intensity and thoroughness of the search.
—Taken from zodiac reading, 2014, "Pluto is in 05 Degrees Scorpio"

in the fragile cosmos
I am often unsure if time heals all wounds
or if the wounds time
the healing

your death was my transformation,
not as in a cocoon's emergence
but a tree's attempt
to grow around obstruction, an uncertain life

it was in part mine, a shared pearl, gift
of painful black sands,
was my forgetting enchantment, how to swim,
fly, or land

was the slow descent into quicksand,
the grotesque question
of what to do with this "now"
we are all supposed to praise so much

it appears the blood still moves along the veins:
embers of Pompeii
are not of yesterday (but how to compose poetry
after Pompeii, anyway)

things are still falling and burning
into charred disorder today;
skulls not philosophic but the stuff of walls and homes
philosophy not even the fugitive key to hope

>   *the flesh of ghosts*
>   *the ghosts of flesh*
>   *which more heavy, which more dense?*

on a gravestone in Paris it reads:
"*Je m'ennuie déjà*" (I am bored already)

come, come, let us stitch
promises of pilgrimage against
the *terra nullius,* towards the dark
sea that calls us to embark

and love, love for no night grows younger;
love, until your future is no longer
something you forget.

torchlit

We are part of the endless ground
beneath constructing myths
as we go along. I tell you
how I grew up in the shadow

of northern trees
and ask if you see how constellations
move through us, get trapped
in us, rise

until looking at the sky
becomes a mirror.
          But here in the world we are
          bones and stink

you say,
          faith and despair
and I think what of what a perfect pair
this is, them being myths too

as we walk, bearing crosses,
torchlit in the night.

There are worldly things, and there are perfect things
thresholds and elevators,
sometimes there are parents and treetops,

the shadows of northern trees.
       These things that bring you up
make you habitual and holy
at once: like the hours,

like our homes, or metaphors for homes;
for there are some we build
and some we take with us.
       You look up at the sky

taut under the moonlight,
and there we are:
lovers,
cross with the stars, looking

for a way to read ourselves
into things, into the face
of all this strange,
vast intimacy.

prayer in patina blue

In the gospel of quantum reality I sing:
        O Earth, sole planet not named after a god,
Who has ever landed softly unto you
What universal language forged on your shores is not cryptic
Which verse of yours can sing to the vanished threads of my people
Why only gravity and not gravitas in your bones
        Not all that is mundane is lost; I look skyward

Often, and imagine not lunar maria as the selenographers do,
        But the Virgin Mary herself, literally sitting
On the moon, looking down at those of us who have only
Looked up in a search for three-dimensional things.
She is there, patiently waiting to escort us into the beyond,
        One by one, and laughing, to keep from crying

My offering: sometimes I imagine it happening
        On bended knee, upon sea floor; I hear not
Voices but the distant sound of ancestors mixed with anemones.
Ending at the beginning, a return
From where we came. Where I will go no one
Will know, perhaps become entangled
        In my hair once overgrown and skin copper

I pray for oxidization, to age graceful as patina,
        An age content to imagine itself in constant
Transformation. Not these vines, snake-like,
Of vehicles pushing into the future,

But the scales of sea-folk and mer-children,
atlases on a new scale,

    Atlantis, imagined in reverse.

Not the pale hue of bodies glued
    To sand attempting colour, but something older and cerulean,
And cold, a place where the cellular becomes spirit,
Returns to its unified self, a combustion
Of water and light, the darkness of the beginning,
The relativity of a seafloor
    Made in the image of our Ichthys.

Where I am from the best prayers
are the nomadic kinds,
take on the shape of anchors,
travel light.

faith 101

above all it has no body, it is akin to the thin line between the here
and now and maybe, it is the willing to leap over many lines, it is
learning how to fly, it is holding your breath, it is the moment of
translation, it is the sound of silence happy with itself, it is mozart,
beethoven, bach, the great cosmologists of life, it is the stars on any
given night, the ghosts of the living also, it is blowing out candles
so others can take pictures, showing up on time, it is also believing
in something beyond time, it is the only constant left, and it is the
chaos, too, the meaning of a wish you make to the tune of flickering
lights, piano keys in a well-ventilated room, it is nervous
improvisation, it is quiet genius, it is loudness of the heart, it is
deliberate passion, reservation gone awry, it is blurry photographs,
paradises made here on earth, it is even what is not paradise always,
the way we unveil, the way we resolve, a revelation of sorts, the
sublime waves of angry rivers, seas, oceans, icebergs of the mind, it
is warm November rain and a cool breeze come June, it is the sky,
and sky-diving leaves, rambunctious rain, the agony and ecstasy, the
sound of classroom chairs, it is something akin to infinity, the
simultaneity of experience, when history comes back and admits
it's been a while, it is a stranger, it is who we know, it is the ghost of
every saint and vice-versa, it is the vice of knowing these verses are
not enough and writing them anyway, it is the language of myth and
metaphor and all other grey matters, it is anything but grey, however,
though it seeks to dissolve all differences, it is a whistle in the dark,
quicksand, thunder, kerygma, enigma, the hallelujah of everything,
the Bible in between the lines, it is a broken compass, it is divergent
woods, roads less taken, it is being taken as a whole by the whole

universe in an instant, the grand scheme of little things, personality
of numbers and fiction of facts, the laws of gravity and the uncut
hair of graves, the beauty of gravitas, poppy fields, stained glass,
that which is essential and thus invisible to the eye, it is the fearing
no evil for thou art with me, it is one foot in front of the other and
alternating, it is I can't go on I'll go on, it is the attempt to attempt at
living regardless it is love regardless it is a regard for those who have
forgotten love, it is trying to continue normally though normal is
something you forget, it is the impossibility of forgetting completely,
the burden of carrying on, it is bearing an impossible cross it is the
possibility of crossing over at any moment it is memory leaking into
the moment it is the moment itself it is living life to its fullest it is the
sometimes strange face in the mirror it is the grace of a tired body the
difference between exist and persist and persevere it is existence per
se it is eyes either opening or closing it is a door or maybe a window
it is a light a flicker a spark and the requisite dark for the aforemen-
tioned it is constellations and the artist and the scientist behind it all
and it is all

my religion is the sea

Sometimes my religion
is the sea. Most days my skin
the colour of burnt sand,
edging the blue.
              I mostly live on the edge of myself.
Other times it is an ocean floor,
its hymns a subterranean lore,
soft and hard, sung
by the *simbis* and sea nymphs:
my beautiful sisters
who will drown

any sailor with the stark anthropology
of their fins and sing deep and long
into rivers of song. They are not metaphors,
              my home is always yonder,
my blood lines are a mix
of what has been washed away
and what was once considered a stain.

Every story I write a handful of light
to stave off the dark
of the ocean, my native land
a dynasty of light hardening into words
bordered by yet another strange

mix of black and blue
skies, black and blue skins
unbreakable as the Atlantic.

Listen to a conch and it will tell you
all you need to know:

stop worshipping what makes
your life impossible, let your prayer
be the effervescent now.

travel tips

Every cry in the vortex
Is the search for *terra firma*

Every repetition the desire
For new earth, as it were

A firmer future, a newer here;
Sand castles that do not disappear

Waves that stay to flirt and play and
Ships that do not scream and birds

That understand freedom and
The freedom to walk forwards

With only the occasional
Glimpse back

To reel back like a fish
Gasping for air

Only to realize the dark
Depths were better anyway

Go forth, dear traveler,
Remembering only this:

If what fills you kills you
Then pray for gills

Or windowsills where you can see stars
Both real and imagined

And if imagining hurts then
Improvise this thing called

Alive
And if living hurts then

Find another frequency
And if you frequently feel

Other
Then settle for the strange

Hallelujah
Of an imperfect self

And if hallelujah hurts
God bless you

And if the blessing hurts
You're on your way

Notes

Credits: The poems, "new world" and "Dante's *Girl at a Latrice, 1862*," appeared in *Ex Nihilo* (Frontenac House, 2010).

"Poemagogy" originally appeared in *GULCH: An Assemblage of Poetry and Prose*, edited by Sarah Beaudin, Curran Folkers, and Karen Correia Da Silva (Tightrope Books, 2009).

Acknowledgements

First and foremost to my parents, sister, and family far and wide: you are my roots, compass, foundation, world.

To my friends, professors, and colleagues: thank you for being my North Star.

To Sonia Sanchez, whose words remain an eternal launch pad, and The Gathering at Keystone College for lighting the way.

To Luciana Ricciutelli and Inanna Publications, for laying the groundwork and making this book a reality—you have my infinite thanks.

To the Canada Council for their generous support and direction in the writing of this book.

And finally to Pavel Kuksa for being my *terra firma* and star-crossed companion—thank you for your love and guidance.

Photo: *Rosanna DeRango*

Adebe DeRango-Adem is a doctoral student at the University of Pennsylvania. Her work has been published in various North American sources, including *Descant, CV2, Canadian Woman Studies/les cahiers de la femme* and the *Toronto Star*. She won the Toronto Poetry Competition in 2005 to become Toronto's first Junior Poet Laureate. In 2008, she attended the summer writing program at Naropa University, where she mentored with Anne Waldman and the late Amiri Baraka. Her debut poetry collection, *Ex Nihilo* (2010) was one of ten manuscripts chosen in honour of Frontenac House's Dektet 2010 competition, using a blind selection process by a jury of leading Canadian writers: bill bissett, George Elliott Clarke, and Alice Major. *Ex Nihilo* was longlisted for the Dylan Thomas Prize, the world's largest prize for writers under thirty. She is also the co-editor, alongside Andrea Thompson, of *Other Tongues: Mixed-Race Women Speak Out* (2010).